FAMOUS ★ FACES

MUSIC FESTIVALS

Danny Pearson

Badger Publishing Limited
Oldmeadow Road,
Hardwick Industrial Estate,
King's Lynn PE30 4JJ
Telephone: 01438 791 037

www.badgerlearning.co.uk

2 4 6 8 10 9 7 5 3 1

Music Festivals ISBN 978-1-78464-373-7

Text: © Danny Pearson 2015
Complete work © Badger Publishing Limited 2015

Publisher: Susan Ross
Project editor: Paul Rockett
Senior editor: Danny Pearson
Editorial coordinator: Claire Morgan
Designer: Jason Billin / BDS Publishing Ltd

Picture credits: antb/Shutterstock.com: 8b; Christian Bertrand/Shutterstock.com: 5, 25b; Bruce Cotler/Globe Photos/ZUMA Wire/Alamy Live News: 16; Everynight Images/Alamy: 23; Juergen Faelchle/Shutterstock.com: 20; Guppyimages/Dreamstime.com: 19; Jonathan Hordle/REX: 14; In Tune/Shutterstock.com: 30b; JStone/Shutterstock.com: 15; landmarkmedia/Shutterstock.com: 12b; Barry Lewis/Alamy: 9t; Ashley Pickering/Shutterstock.com: 18; Prospective56/Shutterstock.com: 8t, 11, 12t, 13t, 24t, 25t, 27t, 28t, 30t; PYMCA/Alamy: 13b; Tolga TEZCAN: 17; Madis Uudam/Shutterstock.com: 21; WENN Ltd/Alamy: 6, 24b; Westmacott/Alamy: 10; Edd Westmacott/Alamy: 22; Wikimedia Commons: 1, 4, 26, 27b, 28–29; yakub88/Shutterstock.com 9b; zhukovvvlad/Shutterstock.com: 19.

Attempts to contact all copyright holders have been made. If any omitted would care to contact Badger Learning, we will be happy to make appropriate arrangements.

FAMOUS ★ FACES

Contents

Vocabulary

Do you know these words? Look them up in a dictionary and then see how they are used in the book.

alternative

festivalgoers

mallet

poncho

producer

spin-off

venues

vice versa

We are going to dive into the world of music festivals. We will take a look at the best festivals in the world and the famous faces they attract.

Festivals have never been so popular! More and more people want to experience and share music away from their homes with hundreds, and sometimes thousands, of other music lovers.

Acts like Taylor Swift, Ed Sheeran, Katy Perry and Pharrell Williams regularly save their best performances for the largest festivals. They sometimes save the best outfits for these shows too.

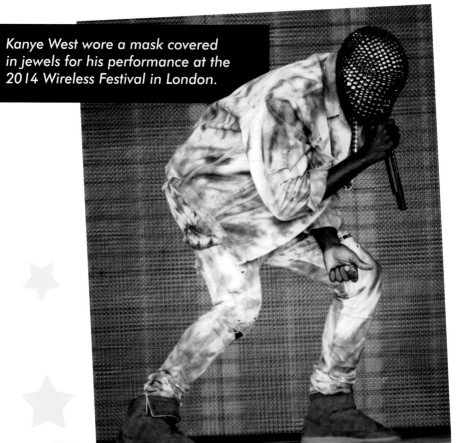

Kanye West wore a mask covered in jewels for his performance at the 2014 Wireless Festival in London.

★★ PROFILE: ★★

Kanye West

Born: 8 June 1977, Georgia, USA

Talent: Rapper, songwriter and fashion designer

Fact: Kanye has designed a pair of adidas trainers and has his own brand of plain white T-shirts that sell for over £100 each!

THE BEST OF BRITISH

The UK is home to some of the world's most famous music festivals. Tickets to some can be very hard to get hold of and can sell out in minutes.

Q unbelievable festival news!

Record ticket sales!

Thousands of music lovers were left disappointed as tickets for the 2015 Glastonbury music festival sold out in record time. 150,000 tickets were snapped up in just 26 minutes!

UK

Glastonbury

The biggest and best-known UK music festival is Glastonbury Festival. Year after year, thousands of music fans make their way to a farm in Somerset to catch their favourite acts.

The population of Glastonbury is usually around 8,000, but when the festival is in town the population jumps to over 200,000!

If you aren't lucky enough to get a ticket, you can always set up a tent in your front room and watch the best bits on the TV or online.

Glastonbury attracts the biggest-selling acts from all around the world. Unfortunately it also attracts the rainy British weather. Wellington boots and a good site for your tent are very important!

Acts who have performed at Glastonbury include:

- ★ **Beyoncé**
- ★ **Daft Punk**
- ★ **Ed Sheeran**
- ★ **Florence and the Machine**

★★ PROFILE:

Ed Sheeran
Born: 17 February 1991, West Yorkshire, England
Talent: Singer-songwriter
Fact: In 2009, Ed played more than 300 live shows in one year!

Glastonbury is not all about the music. You can go there to watch comedy, circus shows and people giving talks about anything and everything.

They have stalls selling foods from all around the world. Name a type of food and it will be there ready and waiting for you to try.

The festival is also very family friendly and provides a mini festival area for babies and children, called the Kidz Field.

★ READING AND LEEDS ★ FESTIVALS

If you are just after music then the Reading and Leeds Festivals are for you. The acts that play at these festivals perform at Leeds one night and Reading the other, and vice versa. This way everyone in Leeds and Reading get to see the same line-up.

Reading and Leeds are often the loudest and craziest festivals. Sleep is seen as a luxury, as parties continue into the night, long after the music has stopped.

Acts who have performed at Reading and Leeds include:

UK

Leeds

Reading

- ★ **Arctic Monkeys**
- ★ **Bring Me the Horizon**
- ★ **Jamie T**
- ★ **Royal Blood**

If you can't get to this festival, much of it can be listened to on the radio or streamed online.

UK

London

The Wireless Festival takes place in London. It is famous for attracting the biggest names in rap and hip hop.

There is no camping allowed at this festival. This means that you have a chance to go back home each night for a nice shower and arrive the next day looking and feeling fresh.

Acts who have performed at Wireless include:

- ★ **Drake**
- ★ **David Guetta**
- ★ **Jay Z**
- ★ **Nicki Minaj**

★★ PROFILE:

Jay Z
Born: 4 December 1969, New York, USA
Talent: Rapper, producer and record label owner
Fact: Jay Z is worth over £500 million. He and Beyoncé married in 2008.

If you prefer your music loud and heavy then Download is the festival for you. It's held each year in Donington Park, Leicestershire, and has hosted most of the world's best known rock and metal acts.

UK

Donington Park

Acts who have performed at Download include:

- ★ **Enter Shikari**
- ★ **Linkin Park**
- ★ **Metallica**
- ★ **Muse**

Band T-shirts are a must at this festival!

★ RADIO 1'S BIG WEEKEND ★

Run by BBC Radio 1, the Big Weekend is the biggest free music festival in Europe. It's held once a year in different places across the UK. Previous venues have included Norwich, Glasgow and Hackney in London.

Radio 1's Big Weekend attracts huge stars and introduces new talent. Acts that have performed at the Big Weekend include:

- ★ **5 Seconds of Summer**
- ★ **Rita Ora**
- ★ **Snoop Dogg**
- ★ **Taylor Swift**

★★ PROFILE:

Rita Ora
Born: 26 November 1990, Pristina, Kosovo
Talent: Singer-songwriter and actor
Fact: Rita's family moved to the UK when she was just a year old. She has been singing from a very early age and is signed to Jay Z's record label.

Hyde Park is one of the biggest parks in London. It holds large events in the summer, with whole afternoons and nights dedicated to concerts by artists such as Kylie and Taylor Swift.

Acts who play at the park usually perform to crowds of over 60,000 people, so make sure you get there early if you want to be near the front!

★★ PROFILE :

Taylor Swift
Born: 13 December 1989, Pennsylvania, USA
Talent: Singer-songwriter
Fact: Taylor is the youngest person to have made the Forbes list of the most powerful women in the world.

CHAPTER 3

FESTIVAL KIT

Let's take a look at the essentials needed for festivals.

- tent ✔
- sleeping bag ✔
- wellington boots ✔
- waterproof poncho ✔ or anorak
- blanket or stool ✔
- umbrella ✔
- bin bags ✔
- sun cream, ✔ sunglasses, hat

Tent

It is a good idea to try and test out your tent before you go to any festival. You need to check for holes and it helps to know how to put your tent up quickly, as spaces away from the festival toilets are taken quickly!

Don't forget to pack the tent pegs and a mallet!

Sleeping bag

It can get very cold at night, even in the summer.

A decent sleeping bag will make sure you have a good night's rest.

Wellington boots

If it gets muddy you will need to be wearing boots. No one enjoys walking around with wet feet.

Waterproof poncho or anorak

When the rain starts to pour, you will be thankful you packed a waterproof poncho or anorak. They come in all different styles.

Blanket or a fishing stool

If you are waiting a long time for an act to come on and don't want to stand or sit in the wet mud, then a small blanket or fishing stool is ideal.

Umbrella

This item can save your festival! In the rain you can stay dry and in the hot sun you can stay in the shade.

Mobile phones often don't work at festivals, so if you and your friends need to split up for a toilet break put your brolly up for them to see. In a huge crowd an umbrella can be spotted from a long distance, so you and your friends won't lose each other.

Bin bags

If you don't fancy carrying a blanket, umbrella and poncho you can simply carry a bin bag in your pocket.

This can be used to sit on **and** can also double up as a waterproof. All you need to do is make three holes in it: one for your head, two for your arms, and then get a friend to slip it over your head!

Sun cream, sunglasses and a hat

If you are lucky enough to have hot weather while at your festival then sun cream, sunglasses and a hat are a must. No one looks good with sunburn!

CHAPTER 4:
FESTIVALS AROUND THE WORLD

★ COACHELLA ★ FESTIVAL

The Coachella Valley Music and Arts Festival takes place in a desert in California, in the USA. It is the festival to go to if you are a celebrity that wants to be seen.

North America

C

Coachella Festival

People like Katy Perry, Kendall Jenner and Justin Bieber like to come here and mix with festivalgoers.

It is America's biggest music and arts event and makes over £60 million a year.

★★ PROFILE:

Katy Perry

Born: 25 October 1984, California, USA

Talent: Singer-songwriter

Fact: Katy Perry holds the record for the longest time spent at number one on the American airplay charts. She spent 46 weeks on the top spot with her single 'Dark Horse'.

BENICASSIM FESTIVAL

The Benicassim Festival attracts all types of music fans with its line-up of indie pop, dance, electro and indie rock. The festival also holds film events and fashion shows.

Europe

It takes place in the town of Benicàssim, in Spain. It is near to several beaches and is very popular with young British festivalgoers who enjoy the hot July weather as well as the music.

B

Benicassim Festival

Acts who have performed at Benicassim include:

- ★ **Arctic Monkeys**
- ★ **Katy B**
- ★ **Jessie J**
- ★ **Ed Sheeran**

★★ PROFILE:

Jessie J
Born: 27 March 1988, London, England
Talent: Singer-songwriter
Fact: Jessie joined the world famous BRIT school at the age of 16. Other BRIT school pupils include Adele and Rizzle Kicks.

★ WARPED TOUR ★

Warped Tour is America's largest travelling music festival. The tour travels all around the USA and beyond. Events have even been held in Australia and Europe.

Many punk rock and alternative bands play at this event and it is a big hit with skateboarding and cycling communities.

The Lollapalooza Festival is held in Chicago, in the USA. It mainly attracts punk rock and alternative bands, but also features some heavy metal, hip hop and dance acts.

North America

Chicago

Europe

Tomorrowland

If you are after something a little different and you love electronic dance music then Tomorrowland in Belgium is the festival for you.

It is the largest annual electronic music festival in the world! It has one of the most impressive stages of all the music festivals and dazzling laser shows.

If you want to treat yourself to a comfortable stay, you and 11 friends can hire a Tomorrowland Mansion.

BOOK NOW
FOR THE
TOMORROWLAND MANSION

Tomorrowland Mansion comes with a big living area, a dining room, Jacuzzi, kitchen and 12 beds.

★★ FACT! ★★

There is also a spin-off festival called TomorrowWor the USA. David Guetta and Skrillex have played her

★ SNOWBOMBING ★

Europe

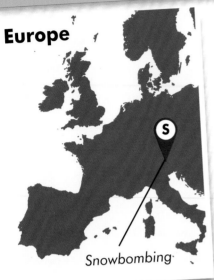

Snowbombing

Snowbombing is a weeklong music and winter sports event held in Austria. It is Europe's biggest snow and music festival. Where else can you watch your favourite acts play alongside the snowboarding greats?

Acts that have performed at Snowbombing include:

- ★ **The Prodigy**
- ★ **Dizzee Rascal**
- ★ **Chase and Status**

Now you are ready for your festival.
Which one will you choose?

Which festival sold out of tickets in less than 30 minutes in 2015? *(page 7)*

★ ★ ★ ★ ★ ★

Name two acts that have played at a Radio 1 Big Weekend. *(page 15)*

★ ★ ★ ★ ★ ★

What is the name of the festival that combines winter sports and music? *(page 30)*

★ ★ ★ ★ ★ ★

Where was Katy Perry born? *(page 24)*

★ ★ ★ ★ ★ ★

Name three essential festival items. *(page 17)*

★ ★ ★ ★ ★ ★

★ INDEX ★